Little Mand

DAY

Science Based Habits to Make Kids

SMARTER, HAPPIER, AND MORE RESILIENT

By Mya and Gianna Gaman

The information in this book is for informational purposes only. No material in this book is intended be a substitute for professional medical advice, diagnosis, or treatment.

First paperback edition July 2023

Book design by Gianna Gaman
Illustrated by Gianna and Alyssa Gaman
Edited by Amy Gaman

ISBN 979-8-9887436-1-3(paperback)
ISBN 979-8-9887436-0-6(ebook)

Published by Little Mandala Books ©
www.littlemandalabooks.com

To my dear reader:
I am so happy to be on this journey with you,
may we continue to grow together.

Author's Note

This book intends to share scientific insights that have been proven to enhance lifespan, health span, and overall life satisfaction. Our aim is to make these valuable lifestyle habits accessible to people of all ages, so everyone can experience the benefits of improved physical and mental well-being. Little Mandala presents these topics in a user-friendly format that outlines the WHAT, the WHY, and the HOW of integrating these science-endorsed habits into our daily lives.

In Part One, we embark on a captivating journey through Little Mandala's day, observing the habits she incorporates into her daily routine. While this guide is suitable for readers of all ages, it is especially designed to resonate with younger audiences. Young children will delight in sharing Little Mandala's journey while learning valuable lessons of how to cultivate happiness, health, and fulfillment in their own lives.

Part Two delves deeper into each daily activity, providing a comprehensive understanding of the science behind them. We explore the compelling research from highly respected institutions and researchers that reveals WHY each habit is so beneficial. Furthermore, we offer simple, actionable instructions to conveniently integrate these habits into our daily routines. They can be introduced one at a time or all at once, in whatever order fits best for each individual.

With this book, we hope to empower readers of all backgrounds to take charge of their well-being and embrace a healthier and happier way of living, supported by the latest scientific findings. By sharing these valuable insights, we aspire to make a positive impact on the lives of people worldwide, contributing to a community of individuals committed to better physical and mental health.

Part One

Little Mandala wakes from her cozy sleep. She opens her eyes and sees her favorite stuffed bunny sitting next to her pillow. Mandala smiles and begins to set her intention for the day. This means she thinks about what she wants to achieve today, and how she wants to feel.

Mandala whispers to herself and her bunny, **"Today, I want to feel strong. Strong enough to cross the monkey bars at recess!"**. She spends a minute in her snug bed imagining herself on the monkey bars, with the warm sunshine on her face, and her friends cheering her on.

Little Mandala finishes her yummy breakfast and then practices her hot chocolate breathing. She closes her eyes and pretends she is holding a cup of tasty hot chocolate in her hands. Mandala takes a big, deep breath in to smell the imaginary drink, **"Mmm ... it smells delicious! I wish I could take a sip of it right now! But wait, this is *hot* chocolate, so I must cool it down before I can drink some!"**. She puts her lips together and slowly breathes out to cool down her hot chocolate. She practices a few hot chocolate breaths until Mommy tells her it is time to go to school.

Little Mandala gets her school bag ready to go. Mandala is happy when she sees her fun lunchbox. She picked it out herself and enjoys getting to use it every day. Mandala fills her colorful water bottle to the top line. She chose the color and decorated it with her favorite stickers. **"I'm so excited to use this!"** Mandala likes to drink out of it during the day and look at her stickers. She skips off to school, ready with all her favorite things.

Little Mandala returns home after a great day at school. Mommy asks about her day, and Mandala is excited to tell her about recess and how she crossed the monkey bars! They chat about the rest of her school day. Mommy asks Mandala's favorite question, *"What did you do that was kind today?"* Mandala is proud to share: **"Today at recess I noticed a friend who didn't have anyone to play with and he was sad, so I invited him to come play monkey bars with us!"** Mandala feels happy that she was kind to her classmate and was able to make him feel better.

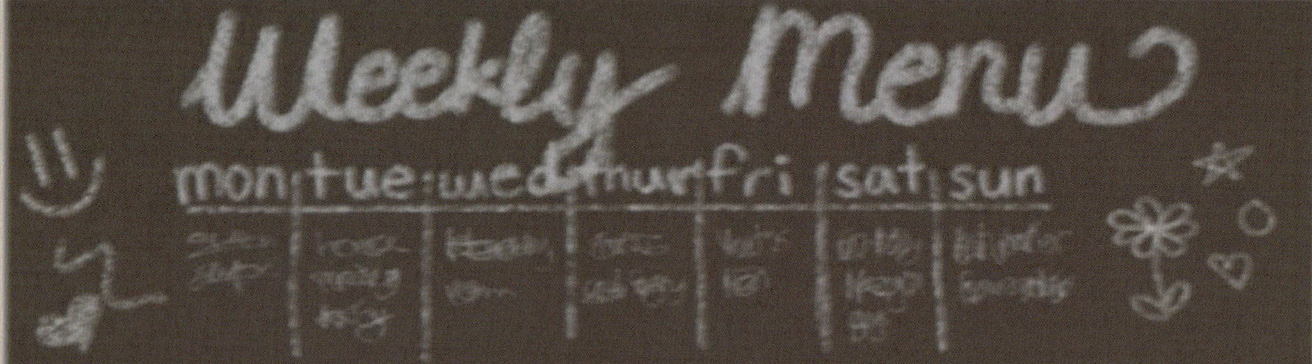

When homework and relaxing time are over, Little Mandala goes to the kitchen to help Daddy with dinner. He gives her a bowl and asks her to pick some strawberries and spinach from their backyard garden. **"Are we having strawberry salad today? Yum!".** Making and eating healthy foods together is a special way that Mandala's family shows that they care about healthy habits and each other.

After clearing up dinner, Mandala's family goes for their relaxing evening walk around the neighborhood. Little Mandala loves breathing in the fresh air, hearing the birds sing, and watching the sky change colors. She smiles and waves at her neighbors and other people she sees during her walk. "Look at the beautiful colors on that tree!" This is one of the best parts of her day. She gets to enjoy being outside with her family while they enjoy the beauty of nature around them.

It is time to shower and get ready for bed when Little Mandala returns home. She enjoys the warm, soothing water and her favorite scented soap. Mandala is proud to save water for the planet by taking shorter showers. She sets her shower timer and relaxes until it is time to get out. **"The timer's done!"**

Fresh and clean in her favorite jammies, Little Mandala giggles when she calls out, "Tuck-in time!" She is laughing because it isn't her bedtime yet, but it is time for everyone's devices to go to sleep. Mandala thinks it is fun to say goodnight to Mommy's and Daddy's phones and computers, and to say that they are getting 'tucked in' for their bedtime.

When it is Little Mandala's bedtime, she crawls into bed and takes out her Gratitude Journal. She thinks about the three best things that she is thankful for today. The first thing she writes about is crossing the monkey bars! She is also grateful that she made a new friend at recess. For the third thing, she gets out her colored pencils and decides to draw instead of write. **"Mmm! Delicious!"** She smiles after drawing the strawberry cupcake she had for dessert and puts away her Journal.

After getting tucked in and saying, **"Goodnight!"**, Little Mandala starts her bedtime meditation. She places one hand on her belly and one on her chest, closes her eyes, and starts to slow down her breathing. She imagines herself under a clear night sky, surrounded by twinkling stars and the soft glow of moonlight. As she continues her deep, steady breathing, she focuses on relaxing her body. She allows herself a slow, satisfying yawn while her clear mind drifts off into dreamland.

Part Two

Neuroscience research reveals that the brain is a *highly plastic organ*, capable of laying down *new neural pathways* and abandoning ones that aren't being used. Furthermore, a ***Stanford Medical School*** professor demonstrated that setting a *clear intention* activates a part of the brain called the prefrontal cortex, thus establishing neural networks that can **facilitate success, relieve chronic diseases, and heal emotional wounds**.[1]

Researchers from ***University of Pennsylvania*** and ***UCLA*** used MRI imaging to visually investigate these changes taking place within the brain: They found *MRI evidence* that parts of the brain involved in positive valuation are *increased when people practice self-affirmation.* These findings suggest that **self-affirmation can be a valuable tool for protecting self-esteem and promoting positive emotions**.[2]

Another ***Stanford*** researcher documented findings that positive self affirmations/intentions can produce a wide range of benefits, including: **reduced stress and anxiety, improved academic performance, increased healthy behaviors, and enhanced relationships.**[3]

(1) Hammer, G. (Host). (2021, January 25). Radiate Intention [Audio podcast episode]. In Radiate Wellness. Radiate Market Media. https://www.radiatemarket.com/podcast/radiate-intention

(2) Cascio, C. N., O'Donnell, M. B., Tinney, F. J., Lieberman, M. D., Taylor, S. E., Strecher, V. J., & Falk, E. B. (2016). Self-affirmation activates brain systems associated with self-related processing and reward and is reinforced by future orientation. Social Cognitive and Affective Neuroscience, 11(4), 621-629.

(3) Cohen, G. L., & Sherman, D. K. (2014). The psychology of change: Self-affirmation and social psychological intervention. Annual Review of Psychology, 65, 333-371.

Morning Intention

Things to do:

- Encourage your child to start the morning with a few deep breaths, and to think about what they would like to achieve for the day.
- Have them imagine what the moment looks like, sounds like, feels like.
- Some children might find it helpful to have a favorite object close by their bed (stuffed animal, toy, picture) that they view when first waking up. This will help place them in the right mindset and serve as a gentle reminder to start the day with intention.

A ***Harvard*** cardiologist has developed a technique to invoke a "*relaxation response*" to *counteract* the stress response ("stress response" = hormone release that leads to physical reactions like heart pounding, gasping for breath, muscles tensing). The *relaxation response* consists of *slow, deep breathing,* which increases activity of the *vagus nerve*, which then signals to the body to **slow down, regulate heart rate, decrease blood pressure, and relax muscles**.[4]

A research team at ***Yale*** performed a mental health study on college students investigating relaxation interventions. They found a mind/body program that incorporated *simple breathing techniques* significantly **improved six measurable outcomes: depression, stress, mental health, mindfulness, positive affect, and social connections**.[5]

A ***Harvard Medical School*** researcher showed that *simple breathing exercises* could **help people sleep better**. Additional research demonstrated how breathing exercises helped insomniac patients **go to sleep 3x faster** than their normal (ten minutes versus thirty minutes), **wake up less frequently** during the night, and **fall asleep faster** when they did wake up at night.[6,7]

(4) Bensen , H. (1976). The Relaxation Response. William Morrow Paperbacks.

(5) Seppala, E., Bradley, C., Moeller, J., Harouni, L., Nandamudi, D., & Brackett, M. (2020, July), Promoting Mental Health and Psychological Thriving in University Students: Randomized Controlled Trial of Three Well-Being Interventions. Frontiers in Psychiatry, 11. doi.org/10.3389/fpsyt.2020.00590.

(6) Bertisch SM, Wells RE, Smith MT, McCarthy EP. Use of relaxation techniques and complementary and alternative medicine by American adults with insomnia symptoms: results from a national survey. J Clin Sleep Med. 2010 Oct 15;6(5):499-506. doi: 10.5664/jcsm.2264.

(7) Tsai, H.J. Et al. (2015, March). Efficacy of Paced Breathing for Insomnia: Enhances Vagal Activity and Improves Sleep Quality. Psychophysiology, Vol. 52, (3); 388–396.

Breathing Exercise

Things to do:

- Try practicing steps of the hot chocolate breath together - feel free to make it playful and enjoy an actual cup of hot chocolate when first practicing.
- Pretend you are holding a cup of steaming hot chocolate in your hands. Next, "smell" the hot chocolate (3-5 second deep inhale). Then, "cool down" the hot chocolate (exaggerated blowing out, build up to 5 second exhale). Repeat this 5 times (total of 6 hot chocolate breaths, or approximately 1 minute).
- Explore other deep breathing techniques. Encourage your child to try utilizing these breathing exercises in the morning, before bedtime, before tests, or any other times that they can use a little relaxation.

Water is an essential nutrient for all bodily functions. Unfortunately, studies show that most children have daily water intake that is lower than the amount recommended by the ***Institute of Medicine***. In those adolescents, *low water intake* was associated with **poor diet quality and physical inactivity**.[8]

Researchers from ***Tufts University*** found that even mild dehydration (corresponding to only 1- 2% of body weight) can lead to *decreases in cognitive function and performance*.[9] Fortunately, ***UK researchers*** proved that children **perform better on memory tests and displayed more sustained attention** on days when they were given 300 mL of water compared to days where no water was provided.[10]

Researchers from ***Boston Children's Hospital*** performed a study investigating a simple intervention: over a span of 25 weeks, they simply made plain water more available in the households of adolescents. They found this simple intervention **decreased sugar sweetened beverage consumption by 82%**, and resulted in a statistically significant **decrease in BMI**.[11] *(BMI = Body Mass Index, measures proportion of weight to height, indirect measure of body fat)*

(8) Park S, Blanck HM, Sherry B, Brener N, O'Toole T. Factors associated with low water intake among US high school students – National Youth Physical Activity and Nutrition Study 2010. J Acad Nutr Diet.

(9) D'Anci KE, Vibhakar A, Kanter JH, Mahoney CR, Taylor HA. Voluntary dehydration and cognitive performance in trained college athletes. Percept Mot Skills. 2009;109:251–269.

(10) Edmonds CJ, Jeffes B. Does having a drink help you think? 6–7-Year-old children show improvements in cognitive performance from baseline to test after having a drink of water. Appetite. 2009;53:469–472.

(11) Ebbeling CB, Feldman HA, Chomitz VR, Antonelli TA, Gortmaker SL, Osganian SK, et al. A randomized trial of sugar-sweetened beverages and adolescent body weight. The New England journal of medicine. 2012;367:1407–1416.

Water Intake

Things to do:

- Invest in a reusable water bottle for your child. Consider letting them help choose the bottle, perhaps in a favorite color or design. They may enjoy personalizing their bottle with stickers.
- Lead by example. Model healthy hydration habits by choosing water over soda, juices, and other sugary drinks.
- Make it fun. Try adding variety by infusing fruit, cucumbers, mint (either directly or frozen in cubes).

Human beings are naturally wired to be compassionate - research from ***Harvard University*** has shown that in both children and adults, our *first impulse* is to *help*, *to be fair*, and to *share*.[12] Moreover, a psychology professor from ***University of Pennsylvania*** has found that *connecting with others* in a meaningful way helps us enjoy **better mental and physical health, and speeds recovery from disease**.[13]

A ***University of Michigan*** researcher found that compassion appears to **lengthen our life spans**. Specifically, study participants who reported higher levels of compassion had a **35% lower risk of mortality** than those who reported lower levels of compassion.[14]

A brain imaging study headed by a neuroscientist from the ***NIH (National Institute of Health)*** showed that the *pleasure centers in the brain* (parts of the brain that are active when we experience pleasure), are **equally active when an individual gives money** to charity, as when they are receiving money themselves.[15]

(12) Keltner, D. (2010). The Compassionate Instinct: The Science of Human Goodness. W. W. Norton & Company.
(13) Seligman, M. E., Steen, T. A., Park, N., & Peterson, C. (2005). Positive psychology progress: Empirical validation of interventions. Psychosomatic Medicine, 67(5), 410-417.
(14) Brown, S. L., Nesse, R. M., Vinokur, A. D., & Smith, D. M. (2003). Providing social support may be more beneficial than receiving it: Results from a prospective study of mortality. Psychological Science, 14(4), 320-327.
(15) Moll, Jorge, et al. "The neural basis of human moral cognition." Nature reviews neuroscience 6.10 (2005): 799-809.

Kindness Counts

Things to do:

- Talk to children about kindness and compassion and encourage them to regularly engage in acts of kindness - to others, as well as to themselves.
- Model good behavior by practicing kind acts yourself. Social scientists from Harvard as well as University of California have proven that kindness is contagious.
- Provide opportunities for your family to connect with the community and perform compassionate acts. Volunteer as a family to serve meals, encourage your children to donate toys, clothes, and books they no longer use, help them to write cards or notes to brighten someone's day.

A 2019 study performed by researchers from ***Cornell*** and ***Tufts University*** found that children who ate a diet rich in fruits, vegetables, and whole grains had better cardiovascular health markers, such as **lower blood pressure and cholesterol levels**, compared to children who ate a less healthy diet.[16]

Researchers from ***Harvard University*** have identified that following healthy eating patterns can **reduce the risk of an early death by up to 20%**. Specifically, people who consume a diet rich in whole grains, fruits, vegetables, nuts and legumes have a *lower risk of death from cancer, cardiovascular illness, and respiratory and neurodegenerative disease.*

In 2017, researchers from the ***Royal Children's Hospital*** in Australia found that children who ate a diet rich in fruits, vegetables, and whole grains had a **lower risk of developing depression and anxiety symptoms** in adolescence, compared to children who ate a less healthy diet.[18]

(16) Miller PE, Li Y, Blumenthal RS, et al. The relationship between healthy diet and cardiovascular disease biomarkers in adults in the United States. Journal of the Academy of Nutrition and Dietetics. 2019;119(5):700-711. doi: 10.1016/j.jand.2018.10.004.

(17) Shan Z, Wang F, Li Y, et al. Healthy Eating Patterns and Risk of Total and Cause-Specific Mortality. JAMA Intern Med. 2023;183(2):142–153. doi:10.1001/jamainternmed.2022.6117.

(18) O'Neil A, Quirk SE, Housden S, Brennan SL, Williams LJ, Pasco JA, Berk M, Jacka FN. Relationship between diet and mental health in children and adolescents: a systematic review. Am J Public Health. 2014 Oct;104(10):e31-42. doi: 10.2105/AJPH.2014.302110.

Healthy Eating

Things to do:

- Involve children in food shopping and cooking from an early age to expose them to a variety of fruits and vegetables. Kids are more likely to give a new food a try if they have had a hand in making it.
- Eat meals together as a family when possible. This will allow you to model healthy eating behavior while making mealtime an enjoyable experience that connects the family together.
- Know your audience when educating children about the benefits of healthy eating. Younger children might be excited to learn that carrots help their eyes work better. Older kids might be motivated to eat healthy when they are reminded that a healthful diet may contribute to better performance in school and in sports.

Contact with nature enhances learning in elementary and high school students. ***University of Illinois*** researchers showed that greenness is tied to **improved academic achievement** - specifically, by *improving children's development of self-discipline, intrinsic motivation, increased school attendance, calmer learning environments, and cooperative relationships with teachers and peers.*[19] Moreover, a ***University of Michigan*** researcher showed greener environments led to **increased standardized test scores**.[20]

Another study found that when children had access to green spaces, they reported **lower levels of stress, anger, and aggression, and had improved moods and self-esteem**.[21] Researchers from ***University of Illinois*** who specifically studied children with ADHD (Attention Deficit Hyperactivity Disorder) found that when the children were in nature settings, they exhibited *fewer symptoms of ADHD and had* **increased attention and focus**. They also self-reported feeling **more relaxed and less anxious**.[22]

A paper published by a ***University of Washington*** researcher showed that the "greener" a child's neighborhood, the **less likely their BMI would increase over a 2 year span**.[23] Additional researchers have found many other health benefits from increased exposure to green space, including **protective benefits for children's lung function and circulatory health, and reduced prevalence of myopia** (nearsightedness).[24]

(19) Kuo, M., Klein, S., Browning, H., & Zaplatosch, J. Greening for academic achievement: Prioritizing what to plant and where. Landscape and Urban Planning, Volume 206, 2021, 103962, ISSN 0169-2046.

(20) Matsuoka, R. H. Student performance and high school landscapes: Examining the links. Landsc. Urban Plan., 97 (2010), pp. 273-282.

(21) Attia, D. S., & Kamel, A. M. (2017). Green spaces and their impact on urban residents' wellbeing. International Journal of Environmental Research and Public Health, 14(8), 802. doi:10.3390/ijerph14080802.

(22) Kuo, F. E., & Taylor, A. F. (2004). A potential natural treatment for attention-deficit/hyperactivity disorder: Evidence from a national study. American Journal of Public Health, 94(9), 1580-1586. doi:10.2105/ajph.94.9.1580.

(23) Bell, J. F., Wilson, J. S., Liu, G. C. (2013). Neighborhood greenness and 2-year changes in body mass index of children and youth. American Journal of Preventive Medicine, 44(5), 427-434. doi: 10.1016/j.amepre.2013.01.022.

(24) Ye, T., Zheng, Y., Wang, Y., Xiang, Y., & Wu, M. (2019). Effects of green space on respiratory and cardiovascular health, and circadian disruption in children: A systematic review of epidemiological studies. Environmental Pollution, 244, 915-924. doi: 10.1016/j.envpol.2018.10.043.

Experience Nature

Things to do:

- Start simple - engaging kids in nature doesn't have to be a fancy, organized event. Begin by setting aside a little time for kids to get outside. Even better, join them if you can. Heading outside for a family walk, or visiting a local park goes a long way.
- When driving your kids to school or activities, try to make it device free time. Encourage kids to look out the window and observe their surroundings - for example, colors of trees or shapes of clouds.
- Consider planting a garden together with their favorite fruits, vegetables, and flowers. An indoor herb garden is an option for seasons or climates that don't allow for outdoor gardening.

Scientists from ***Imperial College of London*** have found that the "warm bath effect" is an actual phenomenon: passive warming from a warm shower or bath for as little as ten minutes, between 1-2 hours before sleep, **shortens sleep latency (the amount of time it takes to fall asleep) by approximately *36%*** (approximately *18 minutes* in the average individual).[25]

In addition to falling asleep faster, researchers from ***Harvard Medical School*** also demonstrated via polysomnography evidence that the warm bath group had significantly **improved sleep quality, as well as increased total sleep time and decreased wake time** after sleep onset.[26]

Studies have also found that taking a warm bath before bedtime is a simple and effective way to *promote relaxation*, particularly for individuals with sleep problems or those experiencing high levels of stress. Specifically, they found that a warm bath was associated with **increased feelings of relaxation, reduced muscle tension, and decreased pain perception**, and it might provide a good alternative to pharmacological treatments in highly stressed individuals.[27]

(25) Beatty, E. R., Roach, G. D., Duncan, M. J., & Smith, S. S. (2020). The effects of passive body heating on sleep: A systematic review and meta-analysis. Sleep Medicine Reviews, 49, 101226. doi: 10.1016/j.smrv.2019.101226.

(26) Dorsey CM, Lukas SE, Teicher MH, Harper D, Winkelman JW, Cunningham SL, Satlin A. Effects of passive body heating on the sleep of older female insomniacs. J Geriatr Psychiatry Neurol. 1996 Apr;9(2):83-90. doi: 10.1177/089198879600900203. PMID: 8736588.

(27) Doughty, J., & Wahler, V. (2020). Hydrotherapy. In J. E. Pizzorno & M. T. Murray (Eds.), Textbook of Natural Medicine (5th ed., pp. 316-330.e2). Churchill Livingstone.

Warm Shower

Things to do:

- Make time for a warm shower or bath approximately 1-2 hours before bedtime.
- Make it fun and relaxing by offering favorite scents, colors, and toys as part of the routine.
- Consider a shower timer - there are many fun options available for this, ranging from digital timers with lights and sounds, to simple hourglass sand timers. Providing this will not only give kids a start time and end time, but will also reduce water consumption and encourage environmental awareness.

A ***Harvard*** sleep researcher found that nighttime exposure to light can *disrupt the body's production of melatonin*, a hormone that plays a key role in regulating the sleep-wake cycle. His research shows that light at night is a reason that many people don't get enough sleep. Moreover, researchers have **linked short sleep to increased risk for depression, as well as diabetes and cardiovascular problems**.[28]

Researchers from ***Harvard Medical School*** and from ***MIT*** published a study showing that **exposure to blue light just before bedtime leads to less quality sleep** in terms of *time spent in REM sleep* (a stage of sleep that is important for memory consolidation and emotional regulation). Additionally, **when people are exposed to blue light, they take longer to wake up and are sleepier and less alert** in the morning.[29]

Additional research has demonstrated that *reducing mobile phone* use before bedtime resulted in: **reduced sleep latency** (time to fall asleep was decreased by 12 minutes), **increased sleep duration** (extended by 18 minutes), **improved sleep quality** (a more rejuvenating sleep experience), **reduced pre-sleep arousal** (a calmer and more relaxed state around bedtime), **improved positive affect** (including enthusiasm, pleasure, and engagement), and **improved cognitive function** (increased working memory).[30]

(28) Lockley, S. W., Brainard, G. C., Czeisler, C. A. (2003). High sensitivity of the human circadian melatonin rhythm to resetting by short wavelength light. Journal of Clinical Endocrinology & Metabolism, 88(9), 4502-4505. doi: 10.1210/jc.2003-030570.

(29) Chang, A. M., Aeschbach, D., Duffy, J. F., & Czeisler, C. A. (2015). Evening use of light-emitting eReaders negatively affects sleep, circadian timing, and next-morning alertness. Proceedings of the National Academy of Sciences, 112(4), 1232-1237.. doi: 10.1073/pnas.1418490112.

(30) He JW, Tu ZH, Xiao L, Su T, Tang YX. Effect of restricting bedtime mobile phone use on sleep, arousal, mood, and working memory: A randomized pilot trial. PLoS One. 2020 Feb 10;15(2):e0228756. doi: 10.1371/journal.pone.0228756.

Goodnight, Device

Things to do:

- Make it a habit to turn off screens at least an hour before bedtime. Younger children might respond better to this rule if they are given a chance to say "goodnight" or "tuck in" their devices.
- If you must use screens in the evening, there are many apps and programs that can reduce the amount of blue light given off by your phone, computer, or tablet. Additionally, consider getting blue-light blocking glasses.
- Explore other activities that your children enjoy before bedtime, such as reading a book, performing some relaxing yoga poses, or winding down with bedtime stretches.

A professor from ***UC Davis*** conducted research on the benefits of gratitude practices. Study participants who kept a gratitude journal for ten weeks reported **better physical health, including fewer headaches, less stomach pain, clearer skin, and reduced congestion**. Moreover, his research confirms that **gratitude effectively increases happiness and reduces depression** - study results indicate that practicing gratitude can *enhance happiness levels by approximately 25%!*[31]

Additional research from ***UC Davis*** found a link between gratitude and **lower levels of inflammation**. They found that gratitude is related to *23 percent lower levels of stress hormones (such as cortisol)*, as well as a *7-percent reduction in biomarkers of inflammation.*[32] Likewise, a **USC** researcher reported that benefits of gratitude include **better sleep, more exercise, reduced symptoms of physical pain, and lower blood pressure**.[33]

Additional research conducted at ***UC Davis*** shows that gratitude **improves self-esteem and emotional resiliency**. They studied how gratitude can *help people cope with negative life events* by providing a *sense of perspective, reducing negative emotions*, and *enhancing positive emotions.*[34]

(31) Emmons, R. A., & McCullough, M. E. (2003). Counting blessings versus burdens: An experimental investigation of gratitude and subjective well-being in daily life. Journal of Personality and Social Psychology, 84(2), 377–389. https://doi.org/10.1037/0022-3514.84.2.377).

(32) UC Davis Health. (2018, November). Gratitude is Good Medicine. Retrieved from https://health.ucdavis.edu/medicalcenter/features/2015-2016/11/20151125_gratitude.html.

(33) Fox GR, Kaplan J, Damasio H, Damasio A. Neural correlates of gratitude. Front Psychol. 2015 Sep 30;6:1491.. doi: 10.3389/fpsyg.2015.01491. PMID: 26483740; PMCID: PMC4588123.

(34) Emmons, R. A., & Mishra, A. (2011). Why gratitude enhances well-being: What we know, what we need to know. In K. M. Sheldon, T.B. Kashdan, & M. F. Steger (Eds.), Designing positive psychology: Taking stock and moving forward (pp. 248-262). Oxford University Press.

Practice Gratitude

Things to do:

- Model gratitude behavior – notice positive things during your day, appreciate them, comment on them to your children. Say thank you to show your appreciation for others.
- Encourage your children to keep a gratitude journal, where they can note things that make them feel grateful during the day. This can be a blank journal where they can write or draw, or a journal with pre-written gratitude prompts.
- Keep a box of blank thank you cards or stationary easily accessible and encourage your children to write thank you notes to others.

People who meditate grow bigger brains than those who don't. Researchers at ***Harvard***, ***Yale***, and ***MIT*** have found brain scan evidence that *meditation can alter the physical structure of our brains*. They found that experienced meditators have **increased thickness in parts of the brain that deal with attention and processing sensory input**.[35]

Other researchers from ***Harvard*** demonstrated that mindfulness for 15 minutes each day actually **alters how genes operate**. They found that people who meditated over an eight-week period had a striking **change in the expression of 172 genes**! Specifically, the genes that were affected were those related to **inflammation, circadian rhythms, and glucose metabolism**.[36]

Researchers from ***Harvard, Yale, and MIT*** found results suggesting that higher levels of mindfulness may **promote academic achievement in students**. Being more mindful may boost a student's academic achievement through *increased attentional control, both while learning and during testing.*[37]

(35) Lazar SW, Kerr CE, Wasserman RH, Gray JR, Greve DN, Treadway MT, McGarvey M, Quinn BT, Dusek JA, Benson H, Rauch SL, Moore CI, Fischl B. Meditation experience is associated with increased cortical thickness. Neuroreport. 2005;16:1893–1897.

(36) Bhasin MK, Denninger JW, Huffman JC, Joseph MG, Niles H, Chad-Friedman E, Goldman R, Buczynski-Kelley B, Mahoney BA, Fricchione GL, Dusek JA, Benson H, Zusman RM, Libermann TA. Specific Transcriptome Changes Associated with Blood Pressure Reduction in Hypertensive Patients After Relaxation Response Training. J Altern Complement Med. 2018 May;24(5):486-504. doi: 10.1089/acm.2017.0053. Epub 2018 Apr 4. PMID: 29616846; PMCID: PMC5961875.

(37) Caballero C, Scherer E, West M, Mrazek M , Gabrieli C , Gabrieli J. (2019). Greater Mindfulness is Associated With Better Academic Achievement in Middle School: Mindfulness and Academic Achievement in Youth. Mind, Brain, and Education. 13. 10.1111/mbe.12200.

Bedtime Meditation

Things to do:

- Establish a bedtime meditation routine: Encourage your child to practice relaxation techniques such as breathing exercises, mindfulness, imagery. Explore which methods they find helpful and incorporate these as part of getting ready for bedtime.
- Consider utilizing guided meditation apps: There are many apps available which are specifically designed for children. These can be helpful in keeping young meditators focused and engaged during their practice.
- Set a good example: Cultivate a meditation practice yourself, and discuss the benefits and positivity you gain from it. Consider occasions where you and your child practice together.

Acknowledgements

We extend our heartfelt gratitude to our mom, Amy, for teaching us the value of embracing healthy habits from an early age and for her enthusiasm and support throughout this journey. Her obsession with wellness podcasters was contagious, supplemented with her role as an actual physician bringing medical insights to our work. As an editor and grammar fanatic, her attention to detail elevated our writing style. As a tireless advocate, she nurtured us in ways beyond measure.

We also owe huge appreciation to our dad and brother, who provided steadfast support and unique perspectives on the subject. Recognizing when to give us space, they would often retreat to the basement, playing countless games of pool or table tennis in hushed tones. But when asked, they willingly set aside their paddles to offer candid and non-sugarcoated feedback. Their constructive critiques, although sometimes tear-inducing, have undeniably made this book better.

We want to thank our teachers for instilling a strong foundation, imparting the essential fundamentals, and for sparking the creativity to always explore new horizons. The unwavering support from our family, friends, and community served as a constant source of motivation throughout the process, as their excitement and enthusiasm for our concept fueled our determination.

This book could not have manifest if not for the tireless efforts of those selfless individuals who generously share their time, wisdom, and experiences to uplift the lives of strangers. Likewise, we are dedicated followers of various podcasters, authors, and researchers, who despite being giants in their fields, humbly and tirelessly make complex information relatable to diverse audiences. We thank all of them for their contributions and hope to join them in our own small way with compassion and purpose to better society. They have touched many lives and inspire us to always strive for more.

Printed in Great Britain
by Amazon

26758549R00023